PARES SCALES

For Individual Study and Like-Instrument Class Instruction

by GABRIEL PARÈS

Revised and Edited by Harvey S. Whistler

Published for:

Flute or Piccolo . . . . Parès-Whistler

● Clarinet . . . . Parès-Whistler

Oboe . . . . Parès-Whistler

Bassoon . . . . Parès-Whistler

Saxophone . . . . Parès-Whistler

Cornet, Trumpet or Baritone 𝄞 . . . . Parès-Whistler

French Horn, E♭ Alto or Mellophone . . . . Parès-Whistler

Trombone or Baritone 𝄢 . . . . Parès-Whistler

E♭ Bass (Tuba - Sousaphone) . . . . Parès-Whistler

BB♭ Bass (Tuba - Sousaphone) . . . . Parès-Whistler

Marimba, Xylophone or Vibes . . . . Parès-Whistler-Jolliff

For Individual Study and Like-Instrument Class Instruction
(Not Playable by Bands or by Mixed-Instruments)

RUBANK®

HAL•LEONARD® CORPORATION
7777 W. BLUEMOUND RD. P.O. BOX 13819 MILWAUKEE, WI 53213

Key of C Major
Long Tones to Strengthen Lips

Scale of C

1

Also practice holding each tone for EIGHT counts.

When playing long tones, practice (1) $<$ and (2) $<$ $>$

2

3

4

Copyright, MCMXLI, by Rubank, Inc., Chicago, Ill.
International Copyright Secured

871-47

8

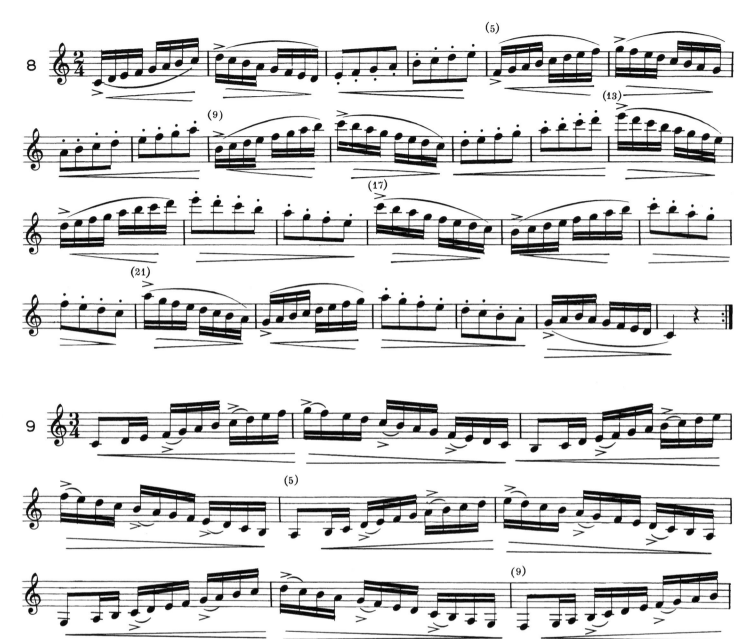

9

Embouchure Studies

10

11

Key of G Major

Long Tones to Strengthen Lips

12

Scale of G

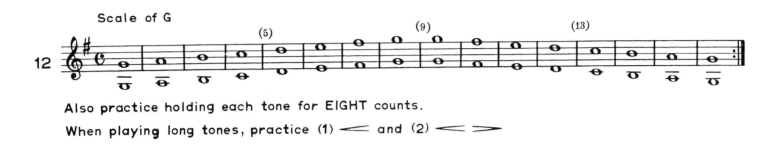

Also practice holding each tone for EIGHT counts.

When playing long tones, practice (1) $\ll$ and (2) $<\,>$

13

14

15

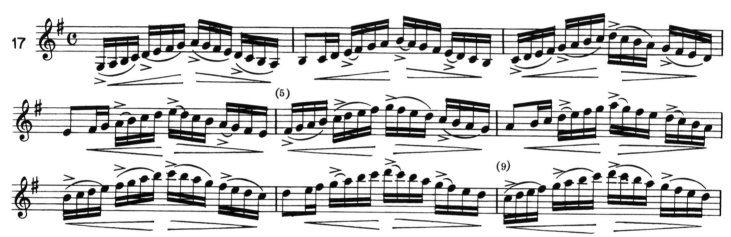

871-47

19

20

21

Embouchure Studies

22

23

Key of F Major

Long Tones to Strengthen Lips

Scale of F

24

Also practice holding each tone for EIGHT counts.

When playing long tones, practice (1) ⟨ and (2) ⟨ ⟩

25

26

27

871-47

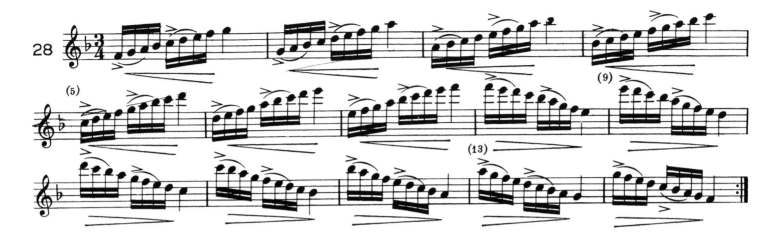

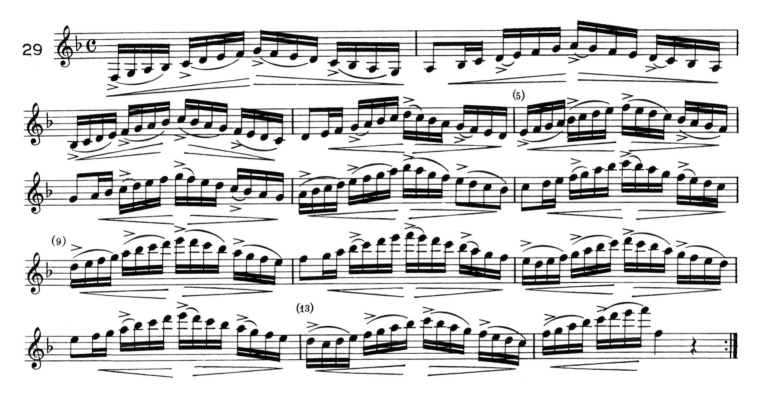

This study may also be played an octave lower   etc.

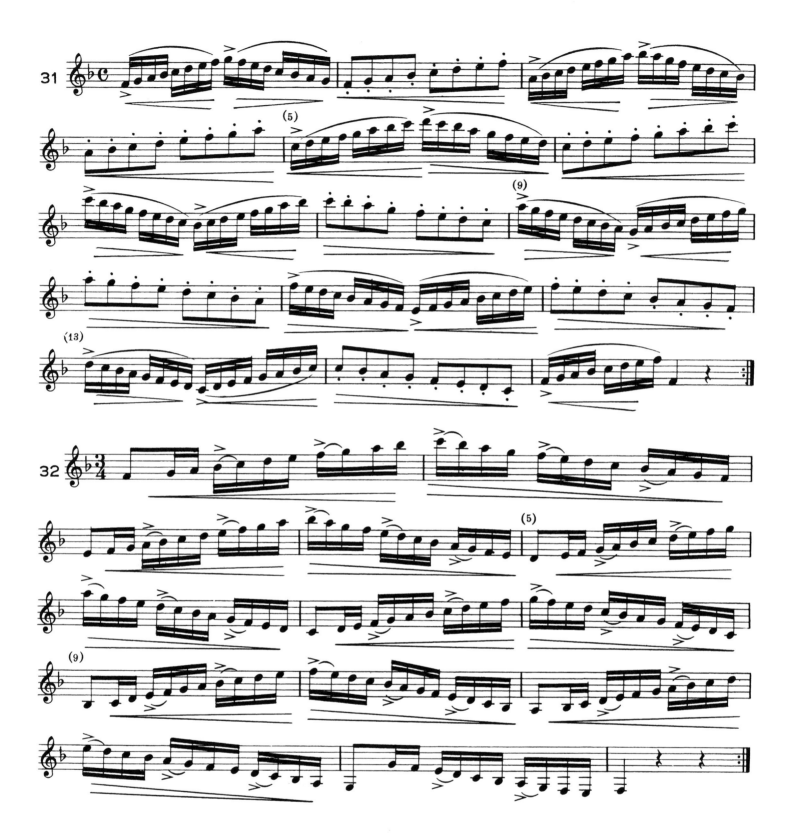

Embouchure Studies

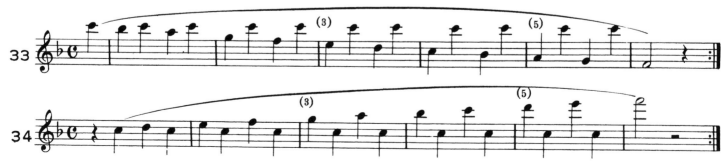

Key of D Major

Long Tones to Strengthen Lips

35

Also practice holding each tone for EIGHT counts.

When playing long tones, practice (1) $\longrightarrow$ and (2) $\longrightarrow$.

36

37

38

39

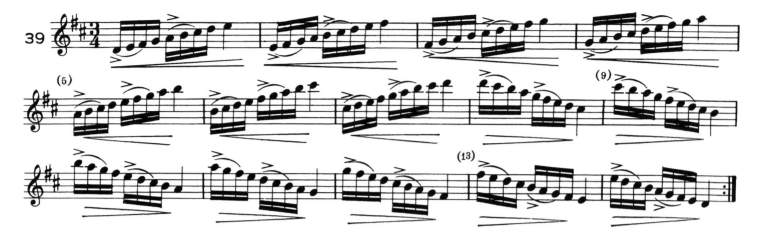

40

41

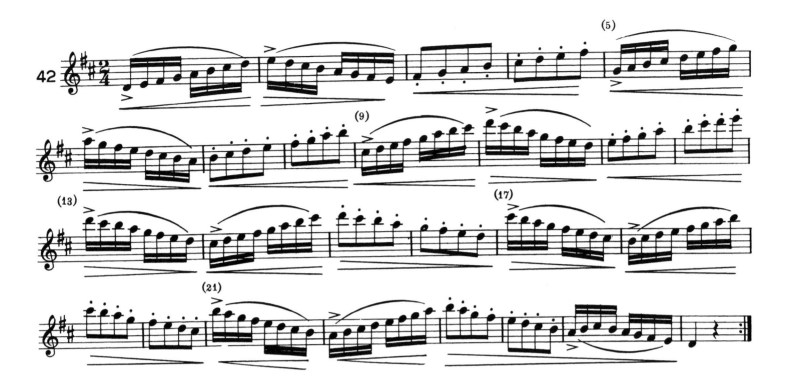

Embouchure Studies

Key of B♭ Major

Long Tones to Strengthen Lips

Also practice holding each tone for EIGHT counts.
When playing long tones, practice (1) $<$ and (2) $<$ $>$.

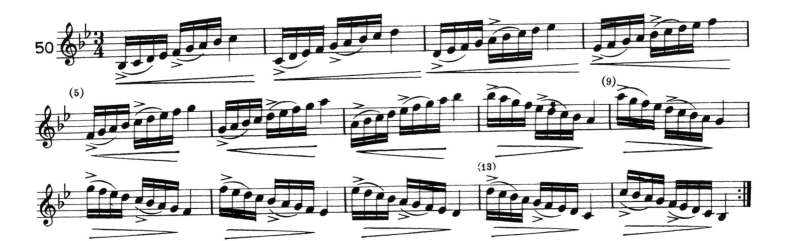

Embouchure Studies

Key of A Major

Long Tones to Strengthen Lips

57

Also practice holding each tone for EIGHT counts.
When playing long tones, practice (1) ⬤⬤⬤ and (2) ⬤⬤⬤ ⬤⬤⬤.

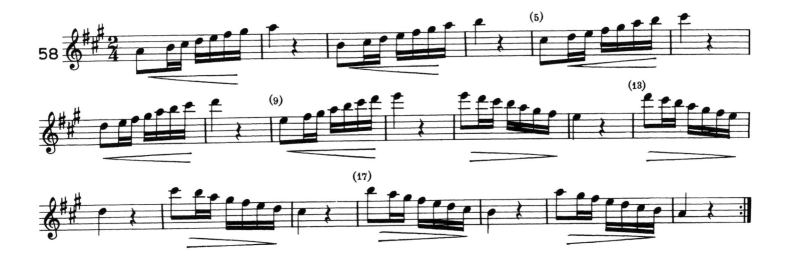

58

59

60

18

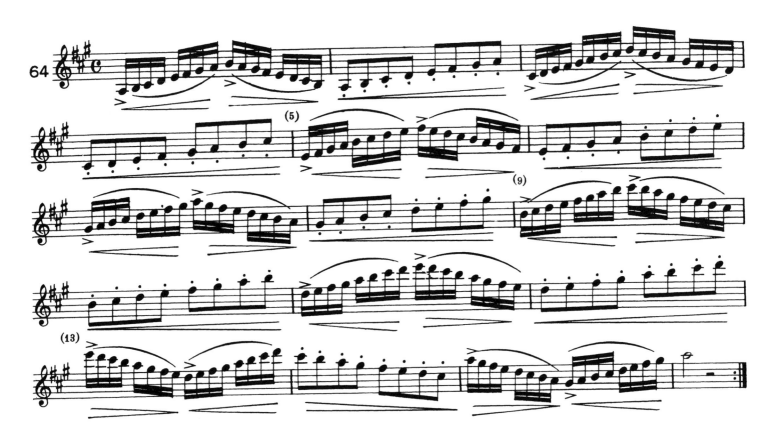

Embouchure Studies

Key of E♭ Major

Long Tones to Strengthen Lips

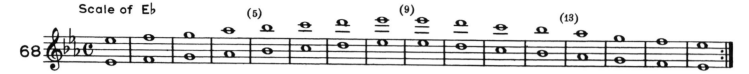

Also practice holding each tone for EIGHT counts.
When playing long tones, practice (1) —◁ and (2) ▷—

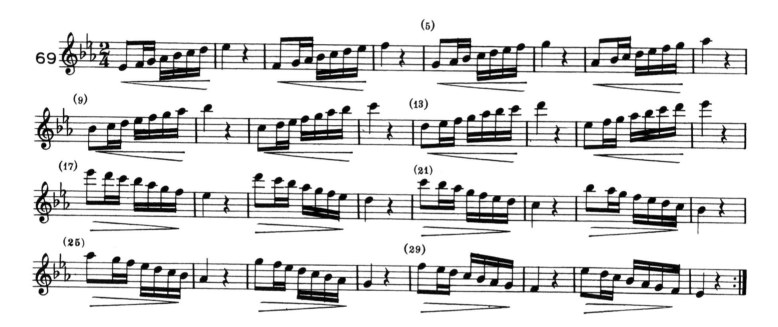

72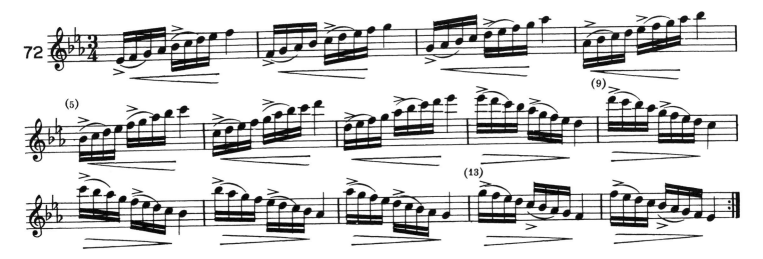

73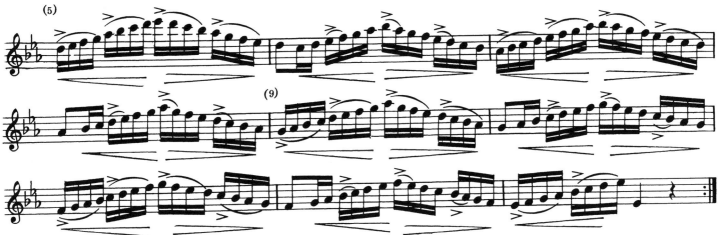

74

75

76

Embouchure Studies

77

78

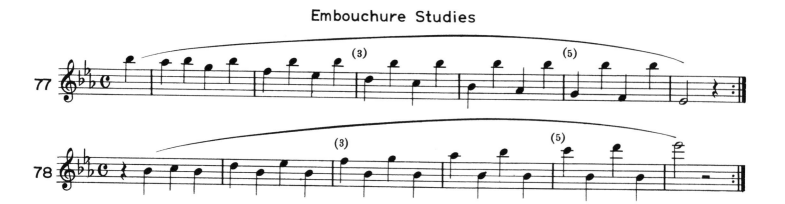

Key of E Major

Long Tones to Strengthen Lips

Also practice holding each tone for EIGHT counts.
When playing long tones, practice (1) $\underset{=\!\!=}{<}$ and (2) $\underset{=\!\!=}{<\!\!>}$.

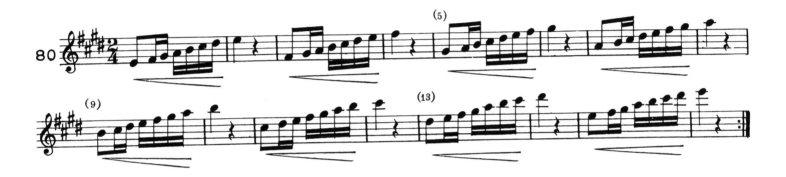

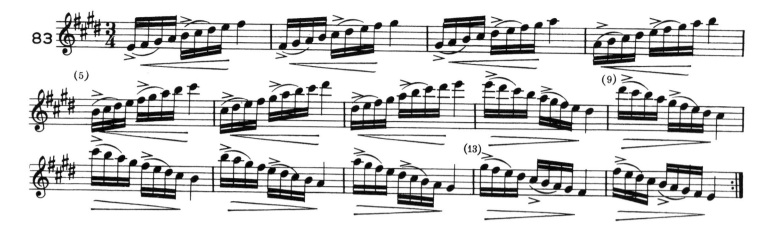

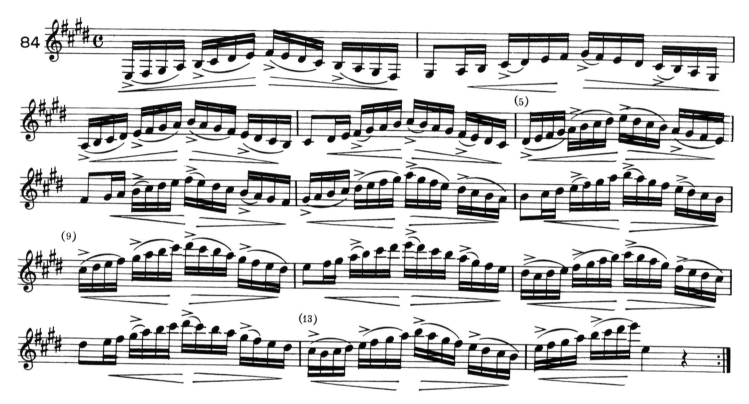

This study may also be played an octave lower   *etc.*

Embouchure Studies

Key of A♭ Major

Long Tones to Strengthen Lips

Also practice holding each tone for EIGHT counts.
When playing long tones, practice (1) ⟨ and (2) ⟨⟩ .

871-47

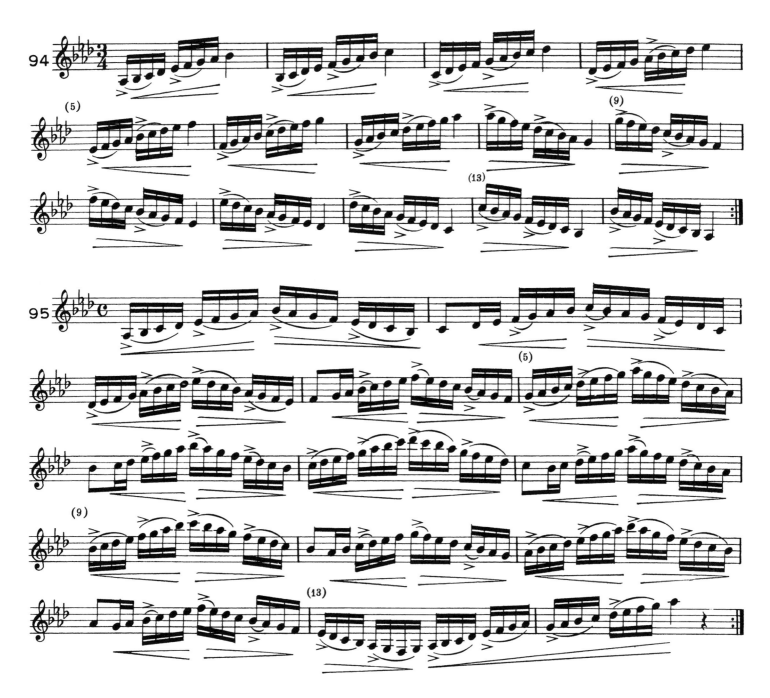

Embouchure Studies

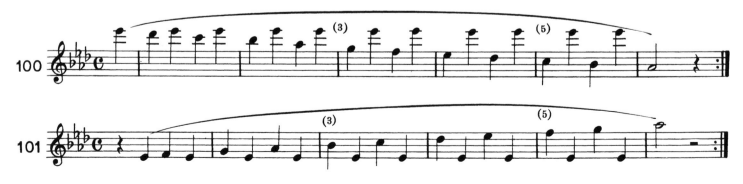

Key of A Minor

(Relative to the Key of C Major)

Long Tones to Strengthen Lips

Scale of A Harmonic Minor

Scale of A Melodic Minor

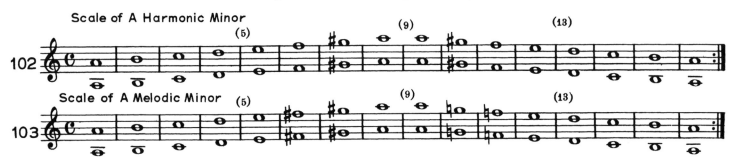

Also practice holding each tone for EIGHT counts.
When playing long tones, practice (1) ⟨ and (2) ⟨⟩

Embouchure Studies

Key of E Minor
(Relative to the Key of G Major)

Long Tones to Strengthen Lips

Scale of E Harmonic Minor

Scale of E Melodic Minor

Also practice holding each tone for EIGHT counts.

When playing long tones, practice (1) ⤙ and (2) ⤙⤚.

Embouchure Studies

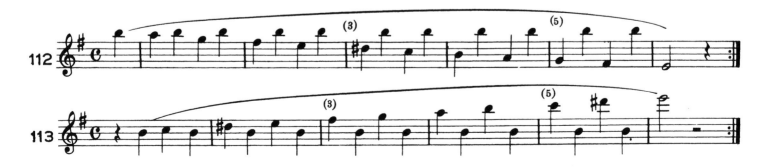

Key of D Minor

(Relative to the Key of F Major)

Long Tones to Strengthen Lips

Scale of D Harmonic Minor

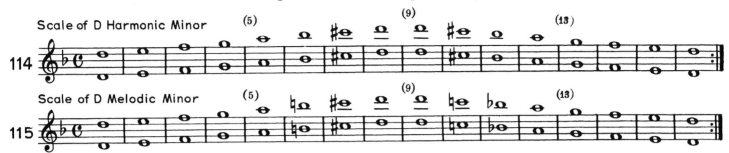

114

Scale of D Melodic Minor

115

Also practice holding each tone for EIGHT counts.
When playing long tones, practice (1) $\diagdown$ and (2) $\diagdown\diagup$.

116

(5)

(9)

(13)

117

(3)

Embouchure Studies

118

119

Key of B Minor
(Relative to the Key of D Major)

Long Tones to Strengthen Lips

Scale of B Harmonic Minor

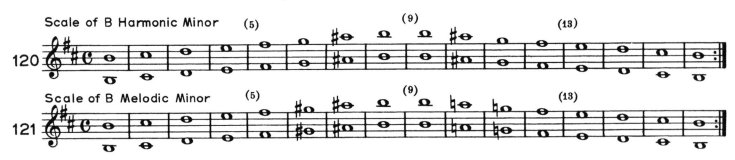

Scale of B Melodic Minor

Also practice holding each tone for EIGHT counts.
When playing long tones, practice (1) $\diagup$ and (2) $\diagup\diagdown$.

Embouchure Studies

871-47

Key of G Minor
(Relative to the Key of B♭ Major)

Long Tones to Strengthen Lips

Scale of G Harmonic Minor

126

Scale of G Melodic Minor

127

Also practice holding each tone for EIGHT counts.
When playing long tones, practice (1) ⫷ and (2) ⫷⫸.

128

Embouchure Studies

130

131

Key of F# Minor
(Relative to the Key of A Major)

Long Tones to Strengthen Lips

132 Scale of F# Harmonic Minor (5) (9) (13)

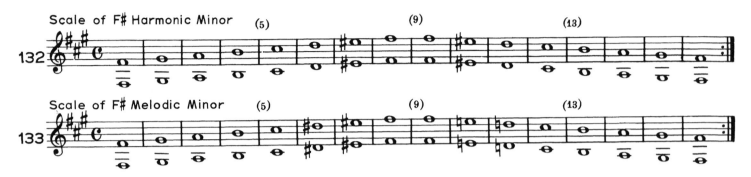

133 Scale of F# Melodic Minor (5) (9) (13)

Also practice holding each tone for EIGHT counts.
When playing long tones, practice (1) ⟨ and (2) ⟨⟩.

134
(5)
(9)
(13)

135
(3)

Embouchure Studies

136 (3) (5)

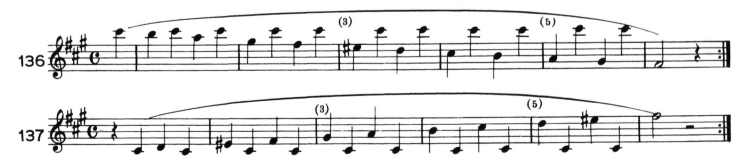

137 (3) (5)

Key of C Minor
(Relative to the Key of E♭ Major)
Long Tones to Strengthen Lips

Scale of C Harmonic Minor

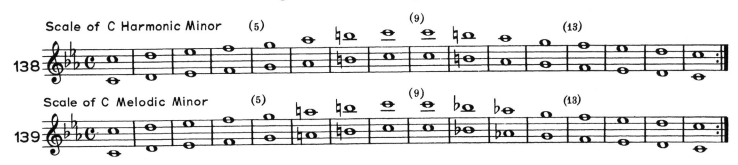

138

Scale of C Melodic Minor

139

Also practice holding each tone for EIGHT counts.
When playing long tones, practice (1) and (2)

140

(5)

(9)

(13)

141

(3)

Embouchure Studies

142

143

Key of C♯ Minor
(Relative to the Key of E Major)

Long Tones to Strengthen Lips

Scale of C♯ Harmonic Minor

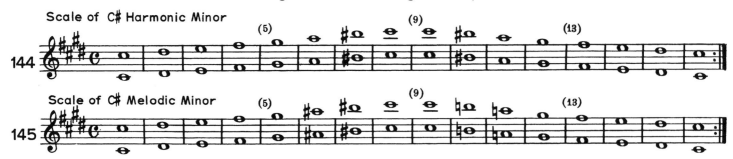

Scale of C♯ Melodic Minor

Also practice holding each tone for EIGHT counts.
When playing long tones, practice (1) $<$ and (2) $<>$.

Embouchure Studies

871-47

Key of F Minor

(Relative to the Key of A♭ Major)

Long Tones to Strengthen Lips

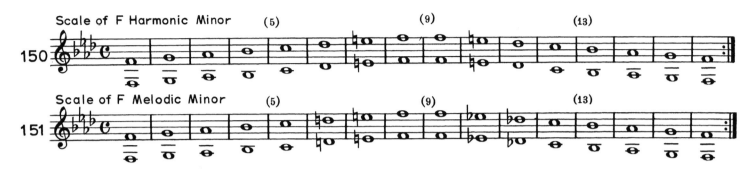

Scale of F Harmonic Minor

150

Scale of F Melodic Minor

151

Also practice holding each tone for EIGHT counts.
When playing long tones, practice (1) < and (2) < >.

152

153

Embouchure Studies

154

155

Major Scales

Harmonic Minor Scales

Melodic Minor Scales

Arpeggios

Major   Minor

Three Octave Chromatic Scales

Four Octave Chromatic Scales

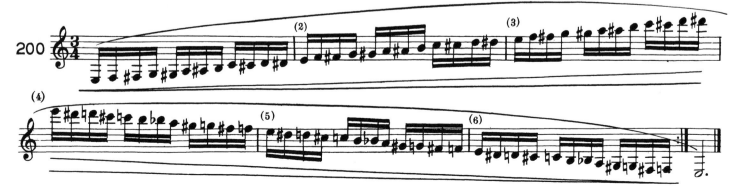

Three Octave Chromatic Scales in Triplets

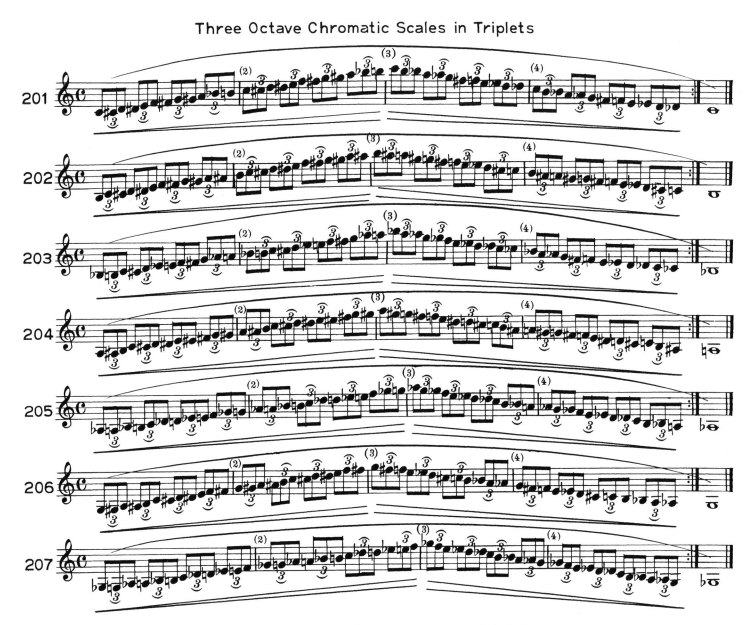

Four Octave Chromatic Scales in Triplets

Studies in Mechanism

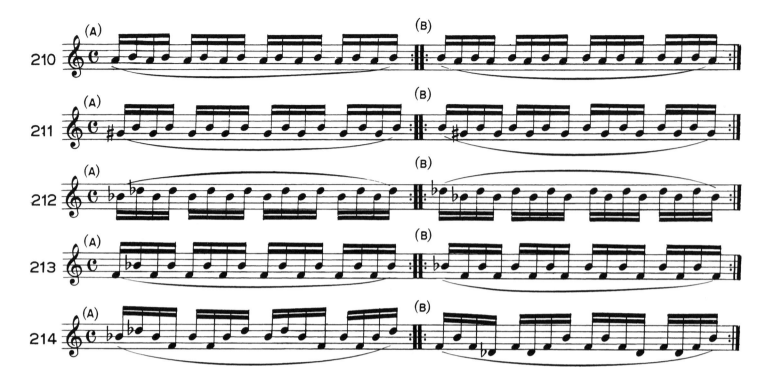

The player not having a G♯-D♯ (A♭-E♭) key on his clarinet will find it necessary in commencing the following studies to produce the first tone with the small finger of the right hand.

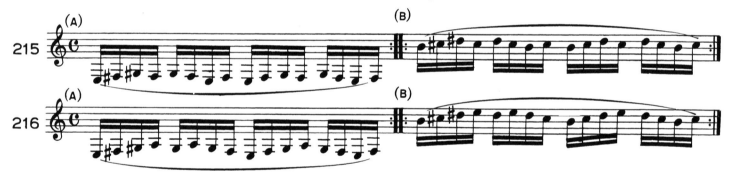

The player not having a G♯-D♯ (A♭-E♭) key on his clarinet will find it necessary in the following study to slide from E to F♯ and from B to C♯ with the small finger of the left hand.

The player not having a G♯-D♯ (A♭-E♭) key on his clarinet will find it necessary in the following study to slide from G♯ to F♯ by dropping the small finger of the right hand in order to permit the playing of the tone E with the left hand.

In the following study the tone D should be produced by using the key for the first finger of the left hand (regular G♯ key) while retaining the fingering of high C.

Right Hand Exercises

Use small finger of Right Hand throughout.

Left Hand Exercises

Use small finger of Left Hand throughout.

Scales in Thirds

Studies in Sixths

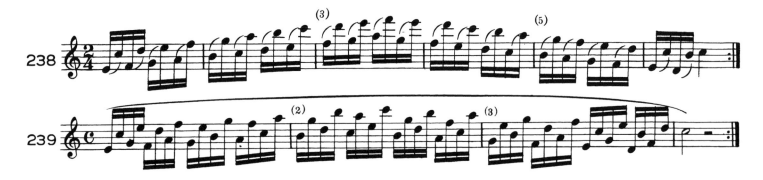

Combined Thirds and Sixths

Triplet Study

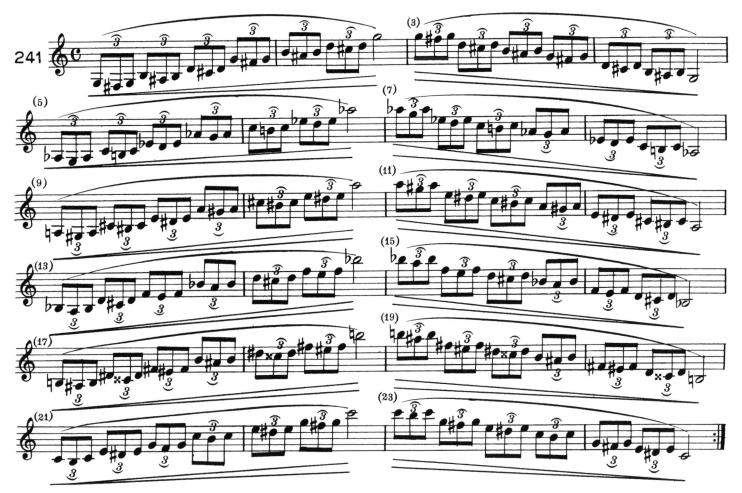

Octave Study